Impressionism Art Kit

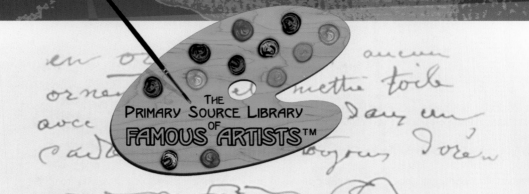

THE
PRIMARY SOURCE LIBRARY
OF
FAMOUS ARTISTS™

PIERRE-AUGUSTE RENOIR

Catherine Nichols

The Rosen Publishing Group's

PowerKids Press™
PRIMARY SOURCE

New York

For Joan Kane Nichols

Published in 2006 by The Rosen Publishing Group, Inc.
29 East 21st Street, New York, NY 10010

First Edition

Editor: Kathy Kuhtz Campbell
Book Design: Emily Muschinske
Photo Researcher: Sherri Liberman

Photo Credits: Cover (background), title page © Christie's Images Limited; cover (left), p. 22 (right) © Musée de l'Orangerie, Paris, France/Bridgeman Art Library Lauros/Giraudon; cover (right) Fogg Art Museum, Harvard University Art Museums, USA/Bridgeman Art Library/Bequest from the Collection of Maurice Wertheim, Class 1906; p. 4 (left) Buhrle Collection, Zurich, Switzerland/Bridgeman Art Library, (right) Musée d'Orsay, Paris, France/Bridgeman Art Library/Lauros/Giraudon; p. 6 © Hulton Archive/Getty Images; p. 8 © Private Collection/Bridgeman Art Library/Phillips, Fine Art Auctioneers, New York; p. 10 (left) © The Barnes Foundation, Merion, Pennsylvania, USA/Bridgeman Art Library, (right) © Reproduced by permission of The State Hermitage Museum, St. Petersburg, Russia/CORBIS; p.12 (left) Museum Folkwang, Essen, West Germany/Bridgeman Art Library/Giraudon, (right), p. 20 (bottom) The Art Archive/Musée du Louvre, Paris/Dagli Orti; p. 14 (left) © Erich Lessing/Art Resource, NY, (right) Musée d'Orsay, Paris, France/Bridgeman Art Library/Giraudon; p. 16 (left and right) © National Museum and Gallery of Wales, Cardiff/Bridgeman Art Library; p. 18 (top) Private Collection/Bridgeman Art Library, (bottom) Metropolitan Museum of Art, New York, USA/Bridgeman Art Library; p. 20 (top) © Francis G. Mayer/CORBIS; p. 22 (left) © Art Resource, NY; p. 24 (left) © The Barnes Foundation, Merion, Pennsylvania, USA/Bridgeman Art Library, (right) Musée de l'Orangerie, Paris, France/Bridgeman Art Library/Giraudon; p. 25 Private Collection/Bridgeman Art Library/Archives Charmet; p. 26 (left) © Edimédia/CORBIS, (right) Musée Renoir, Les Collettes, Cagnes-sur-Mer, France/Bridgeman Art Library/Lauros/Giraudon; p. 28 (left) Galerie Daniel Malingue, Paris, France/Bridgeman Art Library, (right) Private Collection/Bridgeman Art Library/Roger-Viollet.

Library of Congress Cataloging-in-Publication Data

Nichols, Catherine.
Pierre-Auguste Renoir / Catherine Nichols.— 1st ed.
    p. cm. — (The primary source library of famous artists)
Includes bibliographical references and index.
ISBN 1-4042-2765-2 (lib. bdg.)
1. Renoir, Auguste, 1841–1919—Juvenile literature. 2. Painters—France—Biography—Juvenile literature. [1. Renoir, Auguste, 1841–1919. 2. Artists. 3. Painting, French—19th century. 4. Impressionism (Art)] I. Renoir, Auguste, 1841–1919. II. Title. III. Series.
ND553.R45N53 2005
759.4—dc22

                                          2003021951

Manufactured in the United States of America

Contents

Above: *This picture of Pierre-Auguste Renoir was painted by his friend Frédéric Bazille in 1867.*

Left: *Renoir painted eight-year-old Irène Cahen d'Anvers in 1880. During this time, Renoir had to earn his living in Paris by painting pictures of rich people or their children. Irène's father was a banker.*

A Painter of the "Beautiful Time"

Pierre-Auguste Renoir is one of the world's most popular artists. He lived in Paris, France, during the *Belle Époque*, or the "beautiful time," as the French called the period from the late nineteenth to early twentieth centuries. Renoir loved to paint the beautiful and joyful side of life. He showed people having a good time doing such things as dancing, dining, going to the theater, or playing with their dogs. Like his fellow artists who were called **Impressionists**, Renoir often painted outdoors. He painted quickly and painted his works so that they seemed full of light and color. Although Renoir changed his painting style in the 1880s, he is usually linked to Impressionism. A painting style is a certain way or method in which an artwork is painted or made. Renoir painted for more than 60 years. By the time of his death in 1919, he had created more than 6,000 pictures.

This photo of a street in Paris during the 1860s shows the July Column in the Place de la Bastille. Although Renoir was born in Limoges, France, he grew up in Paris. His family moved to Paris around 1844. In the 1860s, when Renoir studied painting, the city was France's center for art. Most of the major art schools were located there, including the famous École des Beaux-Arts, or School of Fine Arts.

Growing Up in Paris

Pierre-Auguste Renoir was born on February 25, 1841, in Limoges, France. He was born into a poor family. He was the sixth of seven children, two of whom died as babies. Pierre-Auguste's father, Léonard Renoir, was a tailor. His mother, Marguerite, was a dressmaker. The Renoirs had a hard time feeding their family. In search of better job opportunities, the Renoirs moved to the city of Paris. The city was about 249 miles (400 km) north of Limoges. Pierre-Auguste was almost three years old.

Pierre-Auguste loved to draw and often filled his notebooks with sketches. Sketches are quick drawings. From 1848 to 1854, he attended a free **Catholic** school. He was a good singer and sang in his school **choir**. Choirmaster Charles Gounod taught Pierre-Auguste to sing. Gounod wanted Pierre-Auguste to become a **professional** singer, but his parents could not afford to pay for the necessary schooling.

Renoir painted this picture, *titled* Still Life of Fruits and Flowers, *in 1889. A still life is a picture of nonliving things.* When Renoir painted pictures on porcelain he often painted them on vases similar to the one seen in this painting. Today none of Renoir's painted porcelain works still exist.

Painting on Plates and Vases

Renoir's school days ended when he was 13. In the 1850s, poor children usually learned a trade when they left school. They became **apprentices**. Renoir's parents saw that he had a talent for drawing. Renoir became an apprentice to a **porcelain** painter. From 1854 to 1858, young Renoir spent his days painting pictures of flowers and **portraits** on porcelain plates and vases. A vase is a tall pot that is used for decoration or for holding flowers.

From this training he learned to draw carefully and to be exact. He also learned good work habits, such as having a plan or a method for working every day. However, Renoir still had dreams of becoming a respected artist of paintings. During his lunch hours, he visited the Louvre, a museum in Paris. He studied works by his favorite artists, such as Antoine Watteau, Jean-Honoré Fragonard, and François Boucher.

Left: *Renoir painted* Woman with a Fan *in 1886. He included a woman holding a painted fan in many of his works.*

Right: *This French fan from the mid-1800s shows a scene of a group of people in the countryside. In 1859, Renoir made his living by painting such scenes on fans and window curtains.*

Studying Art at Last

By 1858, machines were being used to paint pictures on porcelain. The company Renoir worked for went out of business. To earn his living, Renoir painted copies of famous pictures on fans and blinds. Many of these paintings showed fashionable ladies and gentlemen enjoying themselves at picnics or on boat rides. Renoir practiced **technique**. However, he had not yet studied how to create original art.

By the time he was 21, Renoir had saved enough money to take lessons in painting. He enrolled at the Paris **studio** of the Swiss painter Charles Gleyre. He met Gleyre's other students, including Claude Monet, Alfred Sisley, and Frédéric Bazille. These young artists became Renoir's closest friends.

Art Smarts

Renoir practiced painting technique by using his brush in different ways. He also mixed colors to learn what the effects of these colors might be. He especially liked the colors pink and blue and used them to make his pictures look rich and alive.

Above: This paintbox belonged to Renoir. It held his paintbrushes, tubes of oil paint, and a palette. A palette is a wooden tray on which an artist mixes colors of paints.

Left: Renoir's Portrait of Lise, painted in 1867, was shown at the Salon the following year. Certain people who wrote about the 1868 Salon show, such as W. Thore-Burger, liked this painting and wrote good things about it.

Painting for the Salon and *Portrait of Lise*

In 1864, Renoir had a painting accepted by the judges of the Salon in Paris. The Salon was an important art **exhibition**. Having a painting displayed at the Salon was a sign of success for an artist. Renoir's painting, titled *Esmeralda Dancing with Her Goat*, was exhibited at the 1864 Salon. For some reason Renoir destroyed the painting after the exhibition.

Renoir had a girlfriend named Lise Trehot for seven years. Though not much is known about her, Renoir painted her portrait many times. He exhibited a full-length portrait, or a painting that shows the whole body, titled *Portrait of Lise* at the Salon in 1868. It was a great success. **Critic** W. Thore-Burger noticed that Renoir had painted Lise's white dress with a greenish cast, because Lise was in the shade of the trees and grass. Thore-Burger believed that Renoir's painting looked lifelike. The 27-year-old Renoir was making a name for himself.

Above: In 1866, Renoir painted this picture of fellow artist Jules LeCoeur walking in the forest of Fontainebleau. At that time, Renoir often painted his works while outdoors.

Left: Renoir made this picture of his friend, the artist Frédéric Bazille, in 1867. Bazille is shown painting at his easel, which is a tall stand that holds a painting.

Good Friends

Even after Renoir and his friends Monet, Sisley, and Bazille had left Gleyre's studio in 1864, they continued to paint together. They went to the forest of Fontainebleau, an area southeast of Paris, to live and work. Many artists lived and worked in the forest.

Most of these young artists were poor, but they did not care about money. They helped each other by sharing food, lending money, or providing a place to stay. When they returned to Paris, Renoir, Monet, and Bazille shared Bazille's studio for a while. Renoir painted a portrait of Bazille at work. In it he showed one of Monet's paintings hanging on the wall.

In 1870, war broke out between France and Prussia, which later became Germany. Renoir served in the army from August 1870 to March 1871. He did not have to fight in the war. His friend Bazille was not so lucky. Sadly, he died in battle.

Above: *This picture is a small part, called a detail, of La Parisienne. It shows Renoir's brushstrokes of thick paint in the area where the cloth is gathered at the back of the subject's skirt.*

Left: *Renoir painted La Parisienne, or The Parisian, in 1874. The woman in the painting is the actress Henriette Henriot.*

A New Way of Painting

Renoir, Monet, and many other artists were working in a new style. They were more interested in color than in form. These artists tried to paint outdoor scenes as they looked at a single moment and in a certain light.

The Salon turned away many of these paintings because they were so different from paintings of the past. In 1874, Renoir and his friends put on their own exhibition. Critics disliked the new art style. They called it Impressionism. They took this name from *Impression, Sunrise*, which was a painting done by Monet in 1872–1873.

Renoir showed *La Parisienne* at the first Impressionist exhibition. The background, or setting, of the painting is bare except for strokes of color. The brilliant blue dress of the woman in the picture lacks **detail**. But as one follower, Paul Signac, said in 1898, "It is simple, fresh and beautiful. It was painted twenty years ago, but you would think it had come straight from the studio."

Above: *Renoir's* Ball at the Moulin de la Galette *shows dancers at an outdoor dance hall in Paris. Many of these dancers have the faces of Renoir's friends. Renoir painted an ordinary activity and showed the warmth and happiness of the scene.*

Right: *Renoir's 1878 painting* Madame Georges Charpentier and Her Children *appeared in the 1879 Salon exhibit.*

Growing Success

Renoir's fame grew during the 1870s. He also earned more money. Paul Durand-Ruel was an art dealer in Paris. Art dealers are people who buy and sell works of art. Durand-Ruel bought many of Renoir's paintings. Some rich people took an interest in his art. They **commissioned** him to paint their portraits. Then he could pay for his own studio. Renoir painted some of his most famous works during this time. These include *La Loge*, or *The Theater Box*, painted in 1874, *The Swing*, completed in 1876, and *Ball at the Moulin de la Galette*, painted in 1876. Renoir painted several pictures for the Charpentiers. The Charpentiers were wealthy patrons of the arts. Patrons are people who support artists by paying them to create certain works. Madame Charpentier liked to talk with well-known writers and artists, so she invited them to her home. Renoir met many people there who asked him to paint for them.

Above: *In The Luncheon of the Boating Party,* Renoir had his friends pose instead of using professional models. The man at the far left is Alphonse Fournaise Jr., the restaurant owner's son. The woman who is holding the dog is Aline Charigot, Renoir's new girlfriend.

Right: Renoir used this palette, or tray for mixing paint. It has a hole for the thumb, so an artist can hold it while mixing paint and painting a picture.

The Luncheon of the Boating Party

In 1881, Renoir wrote to a friend, "I am doing a picture of a boating party that I have been itching to do for a long time." He knew that it would not be an easy picture to plan. He wrote, "It's a good thing from time to time to attempt something beyond one's powers."

The Luncheon of the Boating Party is one of Renoir's most famous paintings. The scene takes place at the Restaurant Fournaise on the Ile de Chatou, a little island in the Seine River. The lunchtime meal is served outdoors on the landing stage, where people can hire boats. The people in the painting are seen up close, as though the viewer is part of the scene. They are all friends. They are all having a good time. It takes place on a warm, sunny summer day. There is plenty of good food and drink and what looks like good talk. Renoir painted the picture so that the viewer feels as though he or she is enjoying the sunny day along the river, too.

Above: One of Renoir's favorite subjects was young women playing the piano. He painted this picture in 1892.

Left: Renoir worked on The Umbrellas at two different times. He painted the woman and children on the right around 1881. He painted the woman on the left around 1885.

At a Dead End

In 1881, Renoir traveled to the south of France, to Algeria in North Africa, and to Italy. He studied the work of great artists in museums, especially the works of Raphael. He grew unhappy with his own painting. He said, "About 1883 a kind of break occurred in my work. I had gone to the end of Impressionism and I was reaching the conclusion that I didn't know how either to paint or to draw. In a word, I was at a dead end." He tried a new style. Critics call it his dry style. He gave up Impressionism's blurred outlines. He gave objects firmer outlines and a feeling of volume, or mass. In the late 1880s, he created a way of painting that combined Impressionism and his dry style. *Young Girls at the Piano* of 1892 is an example of this style.

Art Smarts

Renoir combined light and rich colors in his new style of painting. He painted the skin on his female figures in a pearly color. He also paid greater attention to detail and to placement of shapes. He painted his subjects so that they appeared to have solid form, as though they had been cut from stone. Renoir also painted in his studio instead of outdoors.

Above: *In 1909, Renoir painted Claude, his youngest son, seen here in a clown suit.*

Left: *Renoir painted this picture of his family in 1896. Pierre, his oldest son, wears a sailor suit and stands next to Renoir's wife, Aline. Gabrielle is seen here with two-year-old Jean. Renoir painted many pictures of Gabrielle and Jean.*

Marriage and Family

Renoir met the seamstress Aline Charigot in 1880 and they fell in love. A seamstress is a woman who makes her living by sewing. For many years Charigot was Renoir's model. In 1885, their son Pierre was born. Five years later, Renoir and Charigot married.

In 1892, Paul Durand-Ruel organized an exhibit for Renoir. Renoir sold many paintings. He could easily afford to support his family. The Renoirs had two more sons. Jean was born in 1894, and Claude was born in 1901. In 1894, Aline's cousin Gabrielle came to help with the children. Renoir, who loved to paint children, painted many pictures of his sons. Claude, whose **nickname** was Coco, had his picture painted in a clown costume when he was eight years old.

This photograph of Renoir was taken in 1885. At that time he was painting in his dry style.

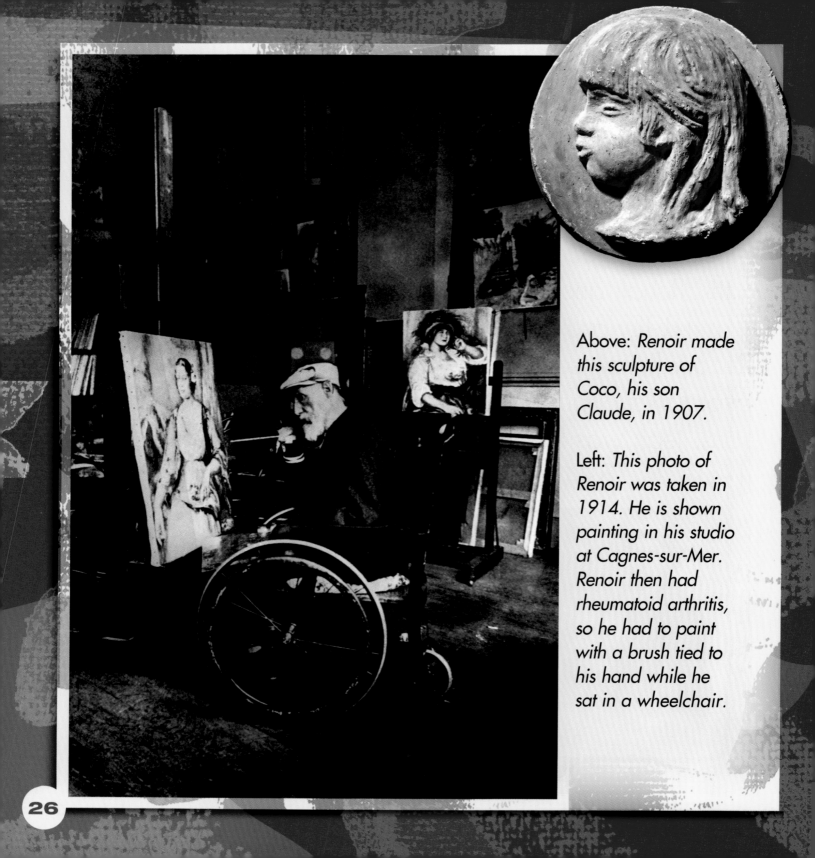

Above: Renoir made this sculpture of Coco, his son Claude, in 1907.

Left: This photo of Renoir was taken in 1914. He is shown painting in his studio at Cagnes-sur-Mer. Renoir then had rheumatoid arthritis, so he had to paint with a brush tied to his hand while he sat in a wheelchair.

A Painful Illness

When Renoir was about 53, he got his first attack of **rheumatoid arthritis**. The illness, which causes swelling and stiffness of joints, grew worse over the years. Cold winters made it harder for Renoir to paint. In 1905, the family moved to Cagnes-sur-Mer in the south of France. It was warmer there than in Paris.

By the time he was almost 70, Renoir could no longer walk because of his illness. He had to use a wheelchair, and he could no longer open his fingers. However, that did not stop Renoir from painting. He had a brush tied to one of his hands or his wrists so that he could still paint.

Renoir also tried to do **sculpture**. In 1907, he made a sculpture of his son Claude. Six years later he worked with a young sculptor named Richard Guino. Renoir gave directions and Guino carried them out. They made several sculptures together.

Above: *This studio of Renoir's was located in his garden in Cagnes-sur-Mer.*

Left: *Renoir painted this self-portrait, or painting of himself, in 1910. Toward the end of his life, Renoir suffered great pain. Jean, his son, once said that the more his father hurt, the more his father painted.*

Full Circle

The outbreak of **World War I** in 1914 saddened Renoir. Two of his sons, Pierre and Jean, were wounded in the fighting. The death of Renoir's wife, Aline, in 1915 also saddened him, but he continued to work. "The pain passes," he once said, "but the beauty remains." In the garden of his house he worked on a huge painting, *The Bathers*. "I shall not die," he said, "till I complete my masterpiece." He completed it in 1918. Critics consider it one of his finest works.

The next year, Renoir was a guest of honor at a party at the Louvre. The museum had bought his 1876–1877 *Portrait of Madame Charpentier*. Renoir was wheeled through the museum he had often visited as a young painter. His life had come full circle. He had become one of the world's great artists and his work was shown in the Louvre. Later that year, on the night of December 3, 1919, Pierre-Auguste Renoir died at the age of 78.

Timeline

1841	Pierre-Auguste Renoir is born in Limoges, France, on February 25.
1844	Renoir moves to Paris with his family.
1854–58	He works as an apprentice, painting pictures on porcelain dishes and vases.
1862–64	He studies with Charles Gleyre and meets artists Monet, Sisley, and Bazille.
1864	Renoir has a painting accepted at the Salon.
1868	Renoir's *Portrait of Lise* is a success at the Salon.
1870–71	Renoir serves in the army during the Franco-Prussian War.
1874	Renoir exhibits at the first Impressionist show.
1875	Renoir finds his first patrons, the Charpentiers.
1881	Renoir travels to southern France, Algeria, and Italy.
1883	Renoir moves away from the style of Impressionism.
1885	Renoir and Aline Charigot's son Pierre is born.
1890	Renoir marries Aline Charigot.
1892	The French government buys Renoir's *Young Girls at the Piano*.
1894	The Renoirs' son Jean is born.
1901	Claude Renoir is born.
1905	The Renoir family settles at Cagnes-sur-Mer.
1910	Renoir needs to use a wheelchair because of his illness, rheumatoid arthritis.
1915	Renoir's wife, Aline, dies.
1919	Pierre-Auguste Renoir dies on December 3.

Glossary

apprentices (uh-PREN-tis-ez) People who learn a trade by working for a person who is already trained.

Catholic (KATH-lik) Someone who belongs to the Roman Catholic faith.

choir (KWY-er) A group of people who sing together.

commissioned (kuh-MIH-shund) To have been asked to do a job.

critic (KRIH-tik) A person who writes his or her opinion about something.

detail (DEE-tayl) The finely or carefully finished parts of a work of art.

exhibition (ek-sih-BIH-shun) A public show of artwork.

Impressionists (im-PREH-shuh-nists) Artists who followed the art movement Impressionism, a style of painting started in France in the 1860s. These artists tried to paint their subjects to show the effects of sunlight on things at different times of day and in different seasons.

nickname (NIK-naym) A name that is used instead of or in addition to a person's real name.

porcelain (POR-suh-lin) A kind of hard, fine pottery that is thin enough to see through when it is held up to the light. Plates, cups, and vases, which are tall containers for flowers, are sometimes made of porcelain.

portraits (POR-trets) Pictures, often paintings, of people.

professional (pruh-FEH-shuh-nul) Referring to being paid for what one does.

rheumatoid arthritis (ROO-muh-toid ar-THRY-tis) An illness that causes swelling of the joints, stiffness, and pain.

sculpture (SKULP-cher) A figure that is carved or formed.

studio (STOO-dee-oh) A room or building where an artist works.

technique (tek-NEEK) A way of bringing about the result one wants in a science, an art, a sport, or a profession.

World War I (WURLD WOR WUN) A war fought from 1914 to 1918. Great Britain, France, the United States, and their friends, who were on one side, beat Germany, Austria-Hungary, and their friends, on the other side.

Index

Primary Sources

Cover. Left. *Young Girls at the Piano*, painted by Pierre-Auguste Renoir around 1892. He painted six versions of this work, the first in 1889. The French government bought the 1892 painting for an exhibition at Paris's Musée de Luxembourg. Today it is in the Musée de l'Orangerie, Paris, France. **Right.** *Self-portrait*, painted by Renoir in 1876 when he was 35 years old. Fogg Art Museum, Harvard University Art Museums, USA. **Page 4. Left.** *Portrait of Mademoiselle Irène Cahen d'Anvers*, painted by Renoir around July 1880. "Little Irène," as she was called, was the eight-year-old daughter of a banker whom Renoir met at the Charpentiers' home. Renoir did the painting during two sittings. **Right.** *Portrait of Pierre-Auguste Renoir* was painted by Frédéric Bazille in 1867 when Bazille, Renoir, and Claude Monet shared Bazille's Paris studio. **Page 12. Left.** *Portrait of Lise* is a painting of Lise Trehot, one of Renoir's models from 1865 to 1872. Here Renoir painted her in the forest of Fontainebleau in 1867. **Page 12. Right.** Paintbox and palette belonging to Renoir. Musée du Louvre, Paris. **Page 16.** *La Parisienne*, painted by Renoir in 1874, is sometimes called *The Blue Lady*. **Page 18. Top.** *Ball at the Moulin de la Galette* is an oil on canvas painted by Renoir in 1876. The painting measures 52 inches (131 cm) by 69 inches (175 cm), which was very large for a picture at that time. The dance hall on Montmartre in Paris was a popular place for young dancers. **Bottom.** *Madame Georges Charpentier and Her Children*, which Renoir was paid to paint in 1878, was a success at the Salon of 1879. The social importance of the wealthy Madame Charpentier and her husband probably contributed to the painting's success. **Page 20. Top.** *The Luncheon of the Boating Party*, which Renoir painted in 1881, shows a merry scene just outside of Paris at the Maison Fournaise, a restaurant and inn, where people could also rent boats to row on the Seine River. **Page 24. Left.** *The Artist's Family*, painted by Renoir in 1896, shows Renoir's wife Aline and their sons Pierre and Jean, Aline's cousin Gabrielle Renard, and a neighbor girl.

Web Sites

Due to the changing nature of Internet links, PowerKids Press has developed an online list of Web sites related to the subject of this book. This site is updated regularly. Please use this link to access the list: www.powerkidslinks.com/psla/renoir/